# TIME SERVED

POEMS

CARLOS CONTRERAS

Published with the generous support of the City of Albuquerque
Public Art Program/Urban Enhancement Trust Fund.

TIME SERVED © 2014 BY CARLOS CONTRERAS

Printed in the United States of America

First print edition March 2014
ISBN 978-0-9910742-1-1

West End Press
P.O. Box 27334
Albuquerque, NM 87125

Back cover art by Jespah A. Torres

Book design by Adam Rubinstein

Set in Solomon and Optima

For book information, see our website at www.westendpress.org.

# CONTENTS

## ACKNOWLEGMENTS

**VETERANO SANCTUARY**

Appeared in *The Black Book*

Gourmet Books, 2008

**TRIGGERS, INVINCIBLE, 2530523**

Appeared in *A Man in Pieces: Poems for My Father*

Gourmet Books, 2013

**FALLING STAR**

Appeared in *Albuquerque Arts and Entertainment*

April 2010, vol.14 no.4

## GRATITUDES

Writing has become living for me. Those that know me best know that it is the way that I never rest and also when I am always at my best—on stage. Life has become a chasing-of-the-opportunity—not for the spotlight or paycheck, but simply for the time to maybe help change a life, even if it's my own. The ones closest to me know this—the ones who have waited for me to be late for dinner, for an appointment, for coffee; the ones who have wished I was at birthdays, graduations, first anythings, they know that this writing mission and journey has always been most important, not because they are less so, but because it is the way that I feel most whole. When I hit that stage—it is in honor of those folks—the ones who know what it is like to be "stage left." This is for you, my parents, my wife, my family: Max and Victoria Contreras, Donna Marlow, Raul and Stephanie Contreras, Angela Tomas and Alyssa Contreras, and "GG."

Writing has become home for me. I have found family outside of the already amazing family I possess. I have found a career with co-workers of a different suit, and one that fits me well. I have found friendship in ways that no other art form would birth. This is also for those folks: Hakim, Colin, Idris, Logan, Damien, Jazz, James, Myrlin, Levi, Jessica, Joe, Rich, Zach, Andrea, Bearface, Cloudface, Cyrus, Sarah K.,

Rusty, Collin, Luke, Leah, Buddha, Zack, Joel, Nikki, JP, Tim, Joe, Kenn, Don, Rich, Manuel, Adam, John and Amanda of West End Press, and so many more. For the owners of Tractor Brewery, Skye and David; for businesses like ArtBar that support all things poetic; and last but not least for my Producer and Director at Triclock Theatre Company, Hannah Kauffman Banks and Juli Hendren. This book is for people like Dr. Shelle Sanchez who have taught me so much, and for the professors pushing me along with work in classrooms near and far, at the university and otherwise: Dr. Vasquez, Dr. Coleman, Professor Romero and the whole Chicano Studies program at the University of New Mexico among them. This is also for every high school English teacher who ever had me visit their school, which is too many to list. Thank you.

This book and the show that will be produced to accompany it are a tribute to the writers I have been blessed to work with in situations and environments of corrections and incarceration. This is for every word released, when the men, women and children themselves have remained captive. This is for the captive audiences that are brave enough to bleed truth onto the page, record their thoughts, and release them into the world. For the JustWrite program and my co-creator Diahndra Grill—this is for us, too!

This is for anyone not named here. I continually thank you for your support and efforts to support all artists. This is a tribute to hard work, not just the hard work of one individual writer but the hard work of a writer's whole community.

Carlos Contreras, Albuquerque, 2014

What happens to a dream deferred?
Does it dry up
like a raisin in the sun?

**Langston Hughes**

# INVINCIBLE

# FOREWORD: 2530523, AKA CHICO CONTRERAS

Sometimes, I can't wrap my head around all of the things I have figured out about myself since my dad sought help. There are certain characteristics in him that I have found in myself, and with his diagnosis of PTSD, it has been easier to figure out how my father's illness has conditioned his way of life, and my own.

The Vietnam War and its lasting effects re-wired my father. The Marine Corps and its training reprogrammed my father. He is the product of firefights, boot camps, and a short-lived childhood. My father grew up in the Marines. At age 18, he was the youngest of three sons. My grandmother was the sole provider for a family that included an abusive, alcoholic husband. Subsequently my father grew up in basically a single-parent household. At 18, looking for guidance, the few and proud seemed like a good start. In retrospect, I would have to say that it probably was.

Sure, my dad maneuvers through difficult things every day, some I will never hear about, but life is like the butterfly effect: had my dad never signed up to be a Marine, he wouldn't have gone, or come back to meet my mother. They wouldn't have married. I wouldn't be here, and this book wouldn't exist.

The price my father paid in witnessing what he did is immeasurable. The fears, anxiety, stress, unrest, and pain my father endures in his journey toward healing are far more harrowing than any bestseller. So in my attempts to share these stories with you, I would like to make it very clear that these stories come out of respect and appreciation. If my father taught me anything, it is that pity is useless. If you don't like your situation, face it head-on and change it. Don't waste time crying or complaining about the way things are—do something about it. My father has "done something about it," his entire life.

When he returned from Vietnam, my father wanted a chance at the freedom he had fought to protect. He was "in pursuit of happiness." He met my mother. He tells stories of working to take her out. They eventually moved into a one-bedroom garage conversion apartment, and they got married. He worked hard to meet my grandfather's approval over the years. He also put in hours to make a life for himself and my mother.

They wanted a family. My parents tried for years to have children, and in the end were given three boys. My mom didn't quite get the fair shake on the girl front. She thought every one of us was a girl up until some point in the pregnancy.

My brother Raul was a girl until the nurses said, "It's a boy." Needless to say, they had to pick a new name.

The full-fledged family my father returned home from Vietnam wanting was well underway. The effects of war were underway as well: the flashback dreams, the distaste for lines, and the fear of crowds my mother told me about. Since he didn't talk about it much, I wonder how long and how hard he dealt with all the rest of it. For how long after the war was sleep really just restlessness? Despite it all, my father focused on raising us, working hard, and doing his best. He was amazing like that.

Upon returning from Vietnam, my dad had two jobs the entire duration of his professional career. He is a loyal man. He retired from Firestone Auto Care, on Seventh and Central, Downtown Albuquerque, after 30 years. It must have been that as a father he knew that life was war too, and the stakes were high. He had started something and he was going to finish it. He liked his situation and wanted to keep it that way. Inside he must have been wrestling with so many things, but outside he dealt with it and pushed through because we were that important to him.

Now looking back, I know that sometimes I must have felt the frustration. I must have sensed and inherited some of the anxieties, because every now and then I feel a little bit of my father inside of me. When I am in crowds, when things get a little too cramped or hot or loud, I feel nervous. I can't control the way I feel when it's really windy or when it rains. I feel anxious on the inside when water beads up on window-panes. It's like something inside me triggers the same pain. The pain of my father, my invincible father.

# TRIGGERS

The dreams
the headaches
stress
back pain
sleeplessness
forgetfulness
fear and restlessness.
They call them triggers.
The doctors
therapists
case workers
and fellow vets.
They all call them triggers.

They all know the triggers
though they're always different,
a subjective affliction.
PTSD preys on the memory,
haunting the sensory.

Tastes smells sounds sights
all manifest as altered evil
to the sufferers.
To the PTSD survivors and the copers,
seeing is not believing.

Things are different than they seem,
and it's scary.

Rain is not just April weather
but the monsoons of Vietnam.
Parks are jungles.
Crowds and lines are boot camp
scenes the soldier wants to forget
but can't.

The returned are reprogrammed
men and women of
a different frequency.
Life is different.
Life holds a different importance
to someone who has undergone this training.
Their experiences have shaped a different life,
and by nature if these men and women have children
some of these ideals are passed along.
The feelings and beliefs of soldiers
can often be found in the hearts and minds
of their sons and daughters.

I now fight a different war,

a smaller one,

a battle I feel well prepared for,

because I too have been trained by a soldier.

## INVINCIBLE

I don't believe in superheroes.
Nobody is invincible.
We all melt at a certain temperature,
and crack under pressure.
So no, I don't believe in superheroes.

For now
I simply have myself:
un-immaculate conception,
a talented yet foiled sense
of misdirection.
I don't see dead people.
I hear emptied souls
sang through song
with notes of no-hope
as interjections.

I don't believe in Kryptonite.
To kill this life
there need be
no injection,
because I
don't believe
in superheroes.

I was born normal.
Son to man and woman
with two sets of hands already full.
There wasn't a free limb to move mountains.
Just one man's mouth
to move three little men.

I convinced myself at an early age:
"Yo, fuck Superman, he ain't even half
as amazing as my dad, so I'll just believe in him."

Sure, Superman could fly
to save fallen babies
from burning buildings
or stop a bank robbery
by turning back time.

But when my dad held you in his arms,
time didn't seem to matter so much.
So I packed a brownbag for lunch.

Because as far as superheroes went,
they didn't outfit a custom tin to showcase mine.
I could always catch my superhero
at the same dad place,
at the same dad time.

I scroll back and quickly rewind:
find him comfortably reclined,
my soft-chested, rough-handed Pops,
feet propped up.
My Bruce Banner,
fighting off the Hulk inside.

Nodding off and trying not to flashback
to the dreams, to the sea of green fatigues.
He fought in Vietnam.

I don't need comic books to show
how war looks or what it means.
I get his confessions that he rarely dreams.
The wishes to revert, remix, and re-live
jungles through the eyes with which only a Dare Devil sees.

When I say, "I don't believe in superheroes,"
perhaps you can begin to understand what I mean.

I mean, life isn't always fantastic.
As a kid, I didn't waste time or money
tugging at the plastic limbs of heroes her and him.
I just wrapped my eyes and ears around the stories of my dad
and asked him:
"Dad, do you believe in superheroes?"

He said,

> "Sure mi jito, I believe in you.
> I believe in your sheer excellence
> And can only imagine what you'll do!"

I said, "Well then Dad,
wouldn't that make you a superhero too?"

He said,

> "No mi jito, sometimes our powers
> leave us when they're through.
> Strength only comes to those
> who need it,
> and I've passed mine
> along to you."

I said, "Really Dad,
then what is it that we do?"

He said,

> "Out of broken pieces,
> we fashion stability, selflessly for others.
> We create infinite possibilities,
> but last and not least,
> we always practice complete humility."

It was then, that I began to believe
this superhero stuff
didn't need to come
with cape and wings.
And about being a superhero,
I learned the very first thing:

I didn't have to believe in superheroes,
but I was a superhero
if one believed in me.

## ALONE

I couldn't imagine,
let alone think.

"How could they imagine,"
he thinks.

We can't imagine what he thinks.
Can't climb into this soldier's mind
like a pair of department issued fatigues.
If only it were that easy.

See,
Marine details make
everything complex,
translate small things
into life lessons.

I used to listen and only half-
pay attention
to the past instances
he took upon himself to mention.

"Don't ever run out of gas.
I won't go pick your ass up."

I'd smile, half laugh
and nod,

then fill up
at the nearest station,
write it off
as the hard-ass in him.

I didn't realize the significance of
never running out of gas again.
Forty plus years ago
he was left vulnerable,
failing hope setting in,
just a soldier and an empty tank.

Just a rifle between him and
back to where he came from.
A laughing gas gauge,
and an AK away from an angry letter
and a folded flag.

He removes himself,
but doesn't leave the vehicle.
The soldier moves off the path
keeps the sleeping beast in his sights,
draped in jungle trying
not to get caught in the sights.

"You never leave the vehicle."

The 18-year-old soldier
in unfriendly territory
tries to stay alive.
Left without time
to reconsider
the hot-headed decision
to jump behind the
wheel and drive.

Halfway between his destination
and nowhere in particular.
Halfway between frustration
and bones shaking in boots.
Halfway between wanting
to be mother's baby again
and hunting like a wolf.
It was the only way
not to be hunted himself.
Halfway to nightfall
and lost prospects,
he digs in deep.

"Hell yeah I was scared,
but there was nothing I could do.

I didn't want to stay in the truck
and be a sitting duck, so I moved."

Alone.
I wonder if he prayed
while he waited?
He knew someone
would eventually find him.
Which side it would be first
became his mind game
while he waited.

18 years must have felt shorter
than that one night
that he managed to stay alive.
Marines towed his truck back to camp
and not without consequence.
My dad hasn't run out of gas since.

Half way between
crazy and amazing
are these products of military training.
Marines were taught to survive in hell
to survive the rain.
But no matter their training,

when soldiers hit the jungle
it wasn't promised they'd last.
A life lost was as simple
as running
out
of
gas.

## 2530523

He became 2530523.
No longer Max Contreras.
To the United States government
he was simply 2530523.

2530523.
No,
it's not a PIN,
or a phone number.
It's the case of one realizing
the severity of hate's hunger.

It's about blood-soaked jungles
and bodies

lain under

bodies

lain under

bodies

lain under
one another.

It's about being
the youngest

of three sons,
and the smallest of
three brothers,
and in our
hearts and minds
there still remains wonder about

bodies

lain under

bodies

lain under

bodies

lain under
one another.

It's about braving monsoons,
with rifle in hand
like perpetual high-noon,
while all the while,
you hear the

( ( ( **BOOOOMM** ) ) )

of bullet-laced thunder.

It's about
being fathered
and watched by eyes
that go to bed,
but never sleep.
Because at bedtime,
a soldier's mind
counts wolves
instead of sheep.

Part of the few and proud
that dug the world out,
when shit got too deep.
Back then, the shit
must have been
waist-high.

Instead of waging war
to waste time,
we warred to waste lives,
and left some men forever changed.
For those who fall,
scrawl their names on a wall.
That shouldn't be enough!
It's not enough for me.

803 dollars a month
for my dad's irreparable
war-inflicted disabilities
does not comfort me!
It's a slap in the face after hugging me.
Money, even if it's clean
can't give my father's dreams back.
Reparations aren't lined with greenbacks.

At 63, post-diagnosis of PTSD,
the best case scenarios are dreams
without the scream
of M-16s.
Truth be told,
when war unfolds
the good Samaritan
never wins.

And so, we're left
with etched names
of the otherwise forgotten heroes.
That's why I've taken
permanent moves to remember you
2530523
Max Contreras.

Knowing I'll only ever be
half the man you are,
and never you.
I love you Papa,
and you're my
hero, too.

# THE WALL

It hit me long after
the two-mile trek to the monument.
I was just in town for the day
and mom figured
it was something I should see.

I didn't think it'd hit me
as hard as an emotional Mack Truck,
a roller coaster ride of my tear ducts.

I could barely compose myself
well enough to shakily hand
a tour guide my chapbook.
They allow you to leave
things there.

They allow you to leave
care packages, stamp and seal
letters. Never before
have I witnessed the alphabet
bear such heavy-hearted happenstance.

Each engraving unique
as the men that were more
than just names,
the simple combination

of coded language that
names are.
Names only tell stories
when people like me ask
questions.
Names are answers:
alphabetical
and ordered
by expiration date.

We the living
are left to realize the weight of war.
I hold my own head in my hands,
alone in a reflective sea of etched letters
feeling like I owe an apology
for existing.

All those children who should have been,
whistled into the wind of a war,
a war that carried away their fathers.
And others who were fathers,
it was for them and my own,
that I left a piece of myself at the wall.

Words from my own hands
on thin paper that lacked
the permanence of granite
were my apology
for breathing.
An explanation
for existence.
A thank you.

An offering of peace that I
hope be unto them.
Had an artist written my father's name
on that wall and in that chapter of history,
I would be a tale untold.
Artistry never owned.
But my dad came home.

And not in a box,
but instead captured by memories
that have in many ways
kept him there
almost just the same.
Standing there
I realized
I'll never be the same.

I was a dream
who now has a name.

A story told
and finished.
A chapter
written.

# HOME

Maybe they don't really die.
Maybe instead they just go home.

Boots unlaced
twice shined
and put away
because they don't need them anymore.

No longer,
and maybe the trip isn't any longer
than an eyelash from eyes
forever closed.
Maybe the trip is the distance
between both edges of a folded flag.

The added total area
of a coffin length
times width
memories multiplied
by laughter,
remembrance.

Maybe they don't really die at all,
but just pack up their things and
just go home.

Albuquerque, Phoenix,
Philadelphia, Los Angeles.
Cities whispered on thin
strips of forever and left up to the wind.

Names of cities
names of soldiers
gliding on sky
riding the night like only they know how,
in stealth,
confident and courageous.
Out of harm's way.

Today we remember, and every morning,
their mothers, fathers, children, and lovers.
We try to forget the last phone call,
the last letter, the folded flag,
21-gun salutes,
and a house that is no longer a home

We find comfort in unbelieving
that ash and shrapnel cradled them in the end.
We imagine the breath of those
they loved the most—
their mothers, fathers, children and lovers
carrying them home.

We imagine they don't die at all,
simply clean their rifles one last time,
give their boots one last shine,
follow the creases of their combat gear
forward,
onward,
upward,
home.

## VETERANO SANCTUARY

*Puro Duranes.*
Dirt and *acequias* behind the house
too much land to know what to do with
the best problem to have
in a city swallowed by concrete.

*Soy de Rio Grande.*

Territorial stomping grounds
for people from
all colors on the palette.
Black, White, Brown.
*Puro*
*Nuevo Mexicanos*
*todos somos*

burnt brown or already there.
I am already here.
Son of the sun,
child of the earth,
screaming my existence at the clouds.

Maybe it will rain
one of these summer days
spent dirtying jeans
and callousing hands,

learning to be a man
the only way my father knew how
to teach us.

Sweat like brail.
Read the salt lines.
Read the hieroglyphics
skin deep.
India ink, tattoos.
Dickies and Ben Davis.
Mad Dogs
and Mad Dog 20/20.
Boones Farm at 14.

Living the dream.

Dying slowly and smiling.
Slow-burning butts
of cigarettes in an ashtray.
Old *Monte* without an air conditioner
and good tunes.

Sunday afternoon
fishbowl cruise
no tint on the windows.
My City.

Definitely not
worried about you, me,
or anyone else,
she's self-motivated.

Seldom motivated to do anything
before tomorrow, next week,
next Wednesday.
But on Sunday nights
she shines like a
Triple Gold Sunflower
100-spoke sunset.

*Veterano* Sanctuary
*Isleta*
*Rio Bravo*
*Barelas*
*Duranes*
*y todo.*

*Soy de tí*
*y el otro.*
*Todos somos*
*locos.*

*Coyotes*
howling.

Full moon,
half-crazy.

Paint job
sun-baked,
half faded
summer nights
leave us half-faded.
*Aye que Burque!*
She's one crazy lady!

Princess puppeteer
stiff shot
Marlboro Light 100 in her clutches
and a cold beer.
Easy to please.

Easy breezy beautiful
*Loca* Girl
Lowrider songstress
cheap-ass in the most
expensive prom dress,
*Todavía* on a cruise,
that's a promise.

One she can keep.
No crossed fingers behind the back.
Just a whisper in your ear
and a lick down the length of your neck.
Cross your heart and hope to die
in a land enveloped in

mountains, sun
sweat and dirt.
*Mariachis, chile*
and *quinceañeras.*
*Chicharrones, margaritas*
and *pachucos.*
*Somos locos*
*hay todos*
*todos somos*

burnt brown or already there.
I'm already here,
waiting for sunset.

# TIME SERVED

## "LIGHTS OUT!"

I wonder often about what goes through the mind of the first-time offender, when the lights go out. The thoughts of more than one sunset, or sunrise, witnessed on the wrong side of cinderblocks and bars? What happens in the thoughts, in the wrestling with sheets and eyelids to not be the first to sleep? What is the reaction to the sounds and scratches in the sheets, in the air, in the wind, the noise nobody can stop when everything is metal and stone? At what point does one mouth the words, or give birth to the wish of wanting to go home? What is the "fresh fish" experience like? Although I cannot say I've been there, I've witnessed the gloss of fear and unpredictability. The killing of that not-so-curious cat, the deer in the headlights, the wanderer on the pod, the one stuck in a corner. I've seen them all, taught them. I feel for those, no matter the offense, who have to realize their situation with time served cold.

## LIFE 101

Life isn't easy.
You can forget about it being nice.

It spends the rent money
to slam some dope,
leaves baggage draped over the
tired bones of a broken home
that has trouble cleaning up
after itself. That's life.

Life is
16 with a bullet,
creased-down Dickies
and crooked finger language.
Life isn't simple.
It's mathematical: divided families,
cause for less and less to add up.

Life's a fight to survive.
It's figuring out
how to make money
and justify making it multiply.
Life is boiling water.
It's sink or swim.

Life is rocks and glass
when you just need something to eat.

It's an expired bus pass
and tired feet.
Life is pennies.
It really doesn't add up to shit.

Life rides the city bus
two grocery bags on each wrist,
purse around the shoulder,
weight of a family in her chest,
eyes forward.

Life's a two-city-block trek
to beat the street lights.
Life is tired.
Hungry.
Beaten.

Life is a song sung
till the throat's
gone sore.

It's a rattle in the chest,
a rail to the veins.
Life is a midnight train
and you the only passenger.

Life is what's at the end of the tunnel,
and being too afraid to find out.
Life is arms riddled with scars
from razor blades glistening with self-doubt.

Life isn't simple,
let alone easy.
Life is crazy.

Life doesn't sing on key.
Life screams at the top of its lungs
in a forest of falling trees.
Nobody around to hear it.
Nobody around to see it.

Life is that kind of story,
Nobody believes it!

Life is a situation of love it or leave it.
It's rolled dice preceding any chance at choosing.
I consider life a no-questions kind of situation,
because I ain't one for losing.

Nobody's laughing.
Life is a joke with the punchline gone missing.

Life is the bruises to prove your presence,
accepting failure and disappointment
like Christmas presents.

It's not getting wrapped up
in the down and out
but picking yourself back up,
each time you fall,
trying to figure this shit out.

## DEPARTMENT OF CORRECTIONS

Working in a correctional facility is not most people's cup of tea, idea of fun, or means of making a living. However, with more than 2 million Americans behind bars, the Department of Corrections is a thriving industry. DOC is a living, breathing entity, with its own laws, unspoken and regulated, and its own codes, made by its inmate populations and the legal system that created it.

The Department of Corrections is self-governed and self-sufficient twenty-four hours a day, three hundred and sixty-five days a year, on its own clock, its own time, its people simply *"doing time."* Within this world there are survivors of all kinds, because behind those bars is a culture. This place that the lucky will never see the inside of is one of the most peculiar and yet *normal* environments on the face of the earth. For many, it is home.

Within the walls of a correctional facility time is lost, passed, wasted, and done. "Doing time." It's a common phrase, inside and out, about what is produced in front of the short-circuit camera. "Doing time." Getting by, over, under, and around just about any rule put in place. An unwritten code of conduct among the incarcerated: the cat and mouse game begins, the us vs. them attitude emerges, constructed along lines of color like at a sporting event or gang fight. Security staff are mostly blue. Inside, there is only security staff and inmates. Aside from those roles, the staff—that's me—we toe the middle line of half an experience, which is what you will get here.

## HEADING WEST

Most days start the same. I-40 west to a street with a changed name, for reasons I've yet to ask, and could care less about since it ultimately leads me nowhere.

Westside Albuquerque. A mesa deserted of hope and ambition, the perfect place to dump 3000 people that everyone else can feel content about forgetting. Those that remember send money, make phone calls, bring bibles or pamphlets, children, or worries; those that still matter sit free on one side of the glass and talk to those barred from society with telephones and cameras. The old booths for viewing are a blast from the past, and nobody talks on pay phones anymore. Well, almost nobody.

The lack of contact in most Supermax, or Supermax-modeled facilities these days is predicated on sterility, impenetrability, and the ability to keep out the contraband, physical or otherwise. The detachment from heartstrings seemingly easier when the phone cords and video screens become not enough for young or expectant mothers, finding less and less gas money to drive out onto west I-40, to a road with a name twice changed.

It is easier for inmates to forget their children's mothers while out on the mesa instead of at tables, at bedsides, at baseball games, or First Grade graduations, when seeing them is almost like a video game, with less excitement. Reality is twisted by visits, twisted into a reality that is not virtual, but instead very, very, real.

## COMMAND CALL

Razor blades,
depending on the day.
Mail, maybe,
a message from the captain:
perhaps beds weren't made in accordance
to the accordion of expectations.
Depending on the oversight
the desired level of diligence
can easily be adjusted.

Discomfort.
Command call.
An upright, out-front, stand in front
of your home line up situation,
where you shut the fuck up
and listen.

It doesn't matter
what you think
made obvious in the tone,
manner and message,
most days, hopefully not all.

Razor blades.
Mail, maybe,
depending on the day.

# HOME

Behind bars is not home. Bars weigh heavy on families' worlds. Mothers are separated from children, men from their wives, and sometimes young people from the only homes they've ever known. Life gets rearranged when a number is assigned, and a unit becomes at the least a temporary resting place, at the worst, a more permanent home.

Just because they are "put away," doesn't mean that those behind bars put things behind them. Instead, the pains fester deep inside, devoid of release. We see it all inside: fights, drugs, sex, suicide. The release of pressure is necessary in any setting, and especially when it's all cinderblock and no sun.

Sons and daughters remember the heavy hands of a father, and blame them for being the reason they beat their own kids. Women replay sexual abuse, succumb to the industry they participate in, before realizing their stepfather's breath matches that of the John that got them into this mess. Memories don't fade. They scratch at the underbelly of sanity. Memories scar, hurt, change, re-wire, and re-anger those dealing with pain alone, in isolation. Time on the pod is wasted trying to forget. Most can't. And we can't blame them.

One can only imagine the demons that chase the thoughts of many of those locked down. The bottles, the needles, the self-sabotage, the violence. All are triggers to a past not worth revisiting. Triggers, therapists call them. Many triggers bear a numbered code in the Department of Corrections.

# CHANCE

Picture this: waiting for days at too young of an age to drive or even walk to a store to buy milk. A drunken haze becomes the way that you remember every day, past the age of single digits, because, well, Daddy did it. Imagine beatings, too brutal to want to remember, still vivid memories, because it's the only answer you have when someone asks you to talk about something in your life that meant *anything*.

Many of these individuals were never given a chance.

When moving from county to state lockup is synonymous in your family with a promotion or graduation, what choice or chance do you have? I am not pointing fingers. I am not calling people bad mothers, bad fathers, or bad seeds of society. Blaming and name-calling help nothing and no one. I am simply asking a question, to shed light on the fact that in this world, things are not fair.

What choice do you have? Cliché as it may be, we have to take off our lenses of judgment, shed the ideas of class, and see socio-economics as a great divider, instead of as a signifier. We are trapped hating each other, and subsequently we have left many of our fellow men and women devoid of even the *chance* at something other than this... something better than nothing.

## DREAM DEFERRED

Questions posed upon a dream
deferred detour
adolescence gone all wrong
over and over
groundhog day now the result
no goals
no prize
nothing won
not even the case.

"She was always on my case, either that or drunk," they
often say,
of mothers,
"He always beat her,"
of fathers,
"I am stupid so why bother,"
of projects.

When one has never experienced the aftermath
of a smile and sweaty brow,
tell me how
at 35 they are supposed to figure it out,
when they *get out*.

Our system lacks the assistance to

transition inmates
from *booking* to a *kick out date*
medicate and isolate
and upon release, they're expected to
be able to relate?
To who?

How do they leave a life
and mind behind
when memories burnt and scarred
can't get out?

No foundation of freedom
or strength of will.
Those things bloodlet in
pre-teen ceremonies
watching mom and dad fix,
meeting different Johns
not being able to keep the lights on.
The explanation:
"That's just the way life is,"

Memories unforgettable as first
dates graduation
*pero*

the flip side of a coin.
The other side of the tracks.
Sad song.
Caged bird.
Broken wings.
Nightmares were all they dreamt,
so how dare anyone ask them to dream?

Upon release
they are a kaleidoscope of hopes
just waiting to be seen.
But to eyes just shown the light
sometimes the only reaction is
"What does it all mean?"

# IN THE CAR

"What's it like?" is the proverbial question that comes up when I present to groups of aspiring writers, teachers, poets. This is always the question when talking about correctional facilities to outsiders. "What's it like?" There is no right answer. There is nothing to say to set the wondering at ease. There are no shock-value stories worthy of placing you on edge.

The reality is most facilities take on their own face. In rural communities, the members of the general population were once members of society outside, otherwise known as the majority population. Before they were inmates, they were shopping at your grocery store, pumping your gas, doing your taxes, serving your drinks, and drinking right beside you.

Rural communities send folks to the "rodeo," and inside they become part of a different community—often a "more comfortable" existence. When entering the Department of Corrections, whether you are security or staff, you must acculturate in order to operate. It is not about changing the system you are in; it's about finding out how you fit in—where and why. If one is able to confront these questions and find comfortable answers, chances are the system will accept you right back. You will be "in the car," so to speak.

In the car, you are "down," cool, trustworthy, ready to roll, and ready to lend a hand. Is this bad? No! If you want to get through to inmates who have done nothing in their lives but be distrusted, berated, battered, and beaten, you must earn trust. No integrity need be sacrificed. Compromise is key. Earning a place to stand doesn't demand an inappropriate favor or anything material. It requires acting and treating others as *human beings*. Acculturation in the department of corrections requires that you learn to be uncomfortable and not show it, exude confidence, demand respect, and get it. Get in the car!

## INSIDE

Everyone sorts through debris, the frightening wreckage. Realizations made along the way of a life strung wayward can be heavy. When life leaves one at the bottom of believing things could be that far down, the result is a turn inward. Lost souls become wrong-way drivers, looking down the barrel of a gun. Memories are not easy to confront. Life becomes a story told in different tongues.

"This time will be different..."

"I just need one more chance..."

"If only I could..."

"If only they would..."

"They just don't understand..."

Stories flame-licked, liquor-soaked or drowned in tears become the road maps that show the ways that confused and troubled souls end up here. Inside. The Department of Corrections is a place that nobody thinks that anyone else can understand, a place of isolation that ironically can follow a release from isolation. The American justice system houses the tick, tick, ticking time bombs. They don't always explode on the inside. Sometimes they get out, and still explode on the inside.

## SIX-SHOOTER

You are
single-barrel
six-shooter
revolver pistols
double-crossed
across the heart
and breast plate.

You are
the thrill of
adrenaline and
good conversation
a point in time
that can't break
a thin line
red though it may be,
maybe, you're all
that ever was and will
be in hiding.
I find myself
beside myself.

Brush strokes
are all that I am
so I remind myself

life is art,
as you are,
a masterpiece.

Masterfully fooling me
to think I am foolish
and otherwise less confident
in these shaky hands that
pen these poems,
I am a long shot lost.
No red slippers
to bring me home.

Not much more
than skin, blood and a bag
of bones,
scribbled on and let go.

Sometimes we need to remind
ourselves to let go.
Caution loves the wind
so throw it out.
Let the fucker sing
Do, Re, Me.
Or scream.

It doesn't matter.
What matters is discovered
when not searching,
when forgetting to
care a little,
for just a little,
surprises present themselves.

When we need to be reminded
we're special
You are.
I am.
We are all
beautiful.

Double-barreled
and four-chambered.
Locked, loaded and
ready realists.
Spinning and clicking,
Russian Roulette dreamers
we are,
hammers back
bent fingers.

## DEPARTMENT OF COLLECTIONS

In this existence, what is it that really stands out, begs to be noticed? This is a question with seemingly endless answers. Inside the Department of Corrections there are lists of common things that we here, on the outside, take for granted. Things that matter. Within those walls, the saying "one man's trash is another man's treasure" rings more true than anywhere else. The incarcerated are not scavengers. They are opportunists, taking advantage of the taken-for-granted. I'm not speaking badly of their conduct or standards because when you walk beyond the secured perimeter of a correctional facility and witness the resourcefulness that takes place—you witness some of the most incredible examples of ingenuity and genius this world has to offer!

The "Department of Collections" is an interesting environment to enter. For those of us who have traded favors, services, or goods, perhaps we can understand it best. You see, as a businessman, with not always the most capital but a whole lot of skills, I can often trade poetry, art, or labor, for print, press, or studio time. I use my business savvy to make sure the lights stay on, my belly stays full, and the roof over my head gets paid for.

On the inside, life is the same. We take for granted how many "businessmen" sit behind bars in our American justice system—those that made money pounding the pavement with their choice of sneaker or boot, bring the same knowledge and determination to the table dressed in shower shoes. Inside, everything has a price. There are stores, although most facilities would like you to think not, and so, yes, there is also inflation, debt, credit, and a "department of collections"— an enterprise with rewards for those with concrete beneath their feet: drugs, sex, money, and status.

What runs the world on the outside, runs the world on the inside. Respect is key to survival. If you choose to buy into that which is outside of your own bank account, level of already-provided entertainment, and or cuisine, there is a good chance you will be dealing with those who have figured things out a whole lot better than you have. There are men and women in our correctional facilities that have realized the American dream. Sure, the picket fence looks different, the family non-nuclear, and the pay scale a little skewed, but capital—and capitalizing—are everything. There are those that will make every attempt and take every chance to make it so.

## DOT-TO-DOT

Sirens, alarms, nightmares, dreams choked and lost, hope extinguished, complacency accepted: They all exist in a world where women and men are walled off, isolated, forgotten. At least we try to forget. But sometimes, we can't drown out the noise, just as they can't drown out the sounds of passing time. Many of them have nothing better to do except make noise, make art, make sense of things, any way possible. We witness this in bodies covered in dot-to-dot tattoos, in vocal chords stretched, in community showers until everyone on the pod tells the song bird to "shut the fuck up," in hands slapped swollen from afternoons of trying to pound a handball through the wall. Behind that wall, existence is at a stand still. Still, the human beings sing, dance, exercise, cry, and wonder about you, too!

## BEAUTY IN THE BEAST

Commissary aside,
there is money and material to be made,
consumed, sought, and created.

Plainly stated,
capitalism is alive and well
among the captive.

Credit.
Collections.
Soups and honey buns
aren't always the commodity.
Nor heroin or cigarettes.
Believe it or not,
poetic genius and art
run blood-rich in the veins
of the Supermax.

Within this culture,
one need not wonder
where the culture's at.
Culture is called dot-to-dot,
collaged chests and backs
ribs and hands.

Fuck it.
Cover the eyelids at that:
"game over"
one word on each
then a laugh and a smile
at the tattooed realization
of life when it bears
its only signs of peace.

Beauty blooms in the belly of beasts.
Look around.
It ain't hard to miss:
cups full of colored pencils,
*old-timers* rocking envelopes for
*short-timers* to send home to their kids.

*Panos* dipped
in sugar, hung to dry,
canvas of a different type.
Bic ballpoints, collage on top
telling the story of a life.

What they don't send home or wear
on their skin, they speak into the world
or pull into themselves until the inside
wears thin.

Tales from a place most
are glad they've never been.
Trauma.
Stress.
Depression.
Poverty.
Loss.
Anger.
Abuse.
Defeat.
Beauty blooms in the belly of the beast.

# FALLING STAR

Falling star
they know you not.
Have yet to discover the
earthquake of man that
lay somewhere between collarbone
and fist.

The boy with razorblades for fingertips,
ready to cut this motherfucker open
from belly button to asshole.
They don't know
the storm they've set abrew.

15: arrested, mistreated, released.
16: arrested, released, beat.
17: arrested, charged, convicted.
18: still serving time, though not the one that did it.

Falling star
they know you not.
They know not the beautiful wound
that has begun
to spread and fester.

When the time comes,
they won't be able to lessen the odds
from one-to-one.

Whoever decides to step inside that cell,
by then it'll be too late to see
that all you needed to do was to figure out
who you were.

Falling star
they know you not.

Never had a chance to figure out the man
that lay somewhere between
eight cylinders of heart and lungs,
a fiery mouth,
and an ass that wouldn't be overrun.

So now you sit
Mack Truck heavy
yard-built beauty of a beast!

Flexing muscles between
pushups and pick-up games of handball.
Closed circuit camera
catches a pit bull showing teeth.

A face saying

       "Try me, try me,
       my house, and everything in between
       you better ask about."

Yet you shake my hand.
We crack jokes and I don't know you
but neither do you
know you.

So daily we flip through
pages of poetry in attempt to figure
out the tick-tick-ticking
that set you up to be a time bomb,
instead of something ready to bloom
beautiful
falling star.

You are an explosion of right
gone wrong.
Daily you write songs
they say

       "listen

            look

                  watch me"

not with careful eyes
but with ones that care.
Poems talk about a father
never there.

About heroin run amok in the city
of your veins,
until it left you on a corner
broke and wishing
on a star far
from anything
you ever considered yourself
to be.

To be or not to,
that is the question
left unanswered.
You remain afraid to write it in
and so we go on in
a calamitous game of
sink or swim,
as reality has its way of
sinking
in.

I came in to work Monday.
You were gone.

You had decided to enterprise on the block,
and get paid instead of getting educated,
and I can't blame you

for resorting to the comforts of the
only things you know.

You are the star fading
somewhere into distance
likened to memories,
as you watch free cable TV,
write your letters,
and take up space.

Falling star
I only hope you find
a place within yourself
that helps you to figure out
the equation
of what was lost,
and all the things that just
don't add up.

You.
Man-made masterpiece,
ticking time-bomb
just waiting to be released,
just waiting
to bloom.

## ABOUT THE AUTHOR

Carlos Conteras is a poet, teacher, and community organizer. He is the author of the chapbooks *A Man in Pieces* and *The Black Book*, both published by Gourmet Books, as well as a National Poetry Slam and Collegiate Slam champion. A founding facilitator in the long-running teen writing program *Voces* at the National Hispanic Cultural Center, Contreras is also co-founder and facilitator for the jail writing program, JustWrite, which connects writers in correctional facilities, universities, and the community in an online forum for writing and performance.

Contreras is one third of the artistic collaborative Urban Verbs, a repertory theater group that combines spoken word, music, and fine art for performances at venues throughout the country. He is the creator of the popular monthly variety show, "I'll Drink to That," and leads event programming at ArtBar as one of the emcees of the weekly show "Untapped." Contreras has been featured in local and regional media, as well as in a video production about Albuquerque that aired on MSN.com. For five years, he worked as an English teacher at the Gordon Bernell Charter School for incarcerated adults in Albuquerque's Metropolitan Detention Center. Contreras currently resides in Albuquerque, where he was born and raised.